I Spy Halloween Book For Kids Ages 2-5

Unleash Your Little One's Imagination with the Exciting I Spy Halloween Adventure!

To Everyone Enjoying the Halloween Spirit This Year!

Hey Parents! Ready to make this Halloween extra special? We've got a spooktacular treat just for you and your little one!

10 FREE Coloring Pages!

Your child will love these exclusive coloring pages filled with friendly monsters, playful witches, and magical Halloween scenes—all inspired by our book. It's the perfect way to keep the Halloween spirit alive and boost creativity!

Getting them is easy:

Just scan the QR code below to instantly download your free pages. It's fast, simple, and sure to bring smiles all around!

Don't wait—unlock more Halloween fun now!
Discover More Halloween Magic Here!

Enjoy The Magic Adventure While
Coloring and Guessing Cute Halloween Things!

Want More Fun & Free Resources?

Unlock 10 exclusive bonus coloring pages, fun activities
all inspired by I Spy Halloween & early access to new books!
It's the perfect way to boost and spark your child creativity!
Simply scan this QR code:

Share Your Experience!

Leaving a quick review helps other parents find this book.
Here's how to do it in 30 seconds:

1. Open your camera app.
2. Point it at the QR code on the right.
3. Boom! The review page opens instantly!

Thanks for being awesome and supporting a small indie publisher like me!
Your feedback makes a huge difference and helps me create more fun books
your kids will love.

Dedicated to all the little explorers
who make every day an adventure.

I Spy with my little eye something beginning with...

Apple

I Spy with my little eye something beginning with...

Bat

I Spy with my little eye something beginning with...

Candy

I Spy with my little eye something beginning with...

Dracula

I Spy with my little eye something beginning with...

Elf

Frankenstein

I Spy with my little eye something beginning with...

Ghost

I Spy with my little eye something beginning with...

Haunted house

I Spy with my little eye something beginning with...

Ice cream

Jack-o'-lantern

I Spy with my little eye something beginning with...

Kitten

I Spy with my little eye something beginning with...

Lollipop

I Spy with my little eye something beginning with...

Mummy

Want More Fun & Free Resources?

Unlock 10 exclusive bonus coloring pages, fun activities all inspired by I Spy Halloween & early access to new books! It's the perfect way to boost and spark your child creativity! Simply scan this QR code:

Your feedback means a lot!

Share your thoughts and help other parents find it!
Scan the QR code below to Leave us a quick review
and let us know What is your impression of the book.

Leaving a quick review helps other parents find this book.
Here's how to do it in 30 seconds:

1. Open your camera app.
2. Point it at the QR code on the right.
3. Boom! The review page opens instantly!

Thanks for being awesome and supporting a small indie publisher like me! Your feedback makes a huge difference and helps me create more fun books your kids will love.

I Spy with my little eye something beginning with...

Nest

I Spy with my little eye something beginning with...

Owl

I Spy with my little eye something beginning with...

Pumpkin

I Spy with my little eye something beginning with...

Queen

I Spy with my little eye something beginning with...

Raven

I Spy with my little eye something beginning with...

Spider

Tombstone

I Spy with my little eye something beginning with...

Unicorn

I Spy with my little eye something beginning with...

Vampire

I Spy with my little eye something beginning with...

Witch

I Spy with my little eye something beginning with...

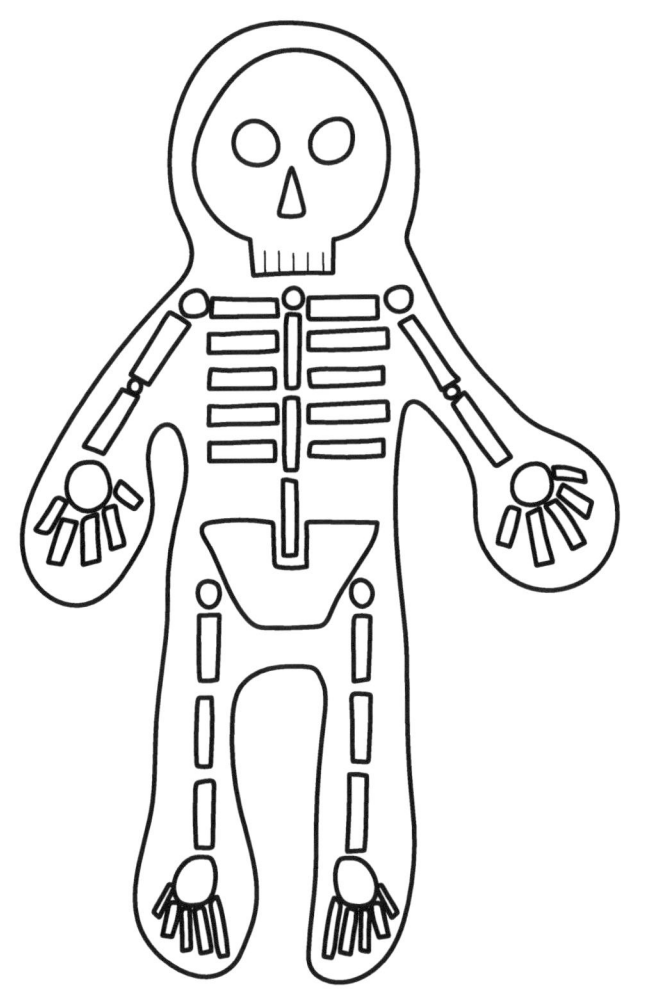

X-Ray Skeleton

I Spy with my little eye something beginning with...

Yarn

Zombie

Practice Writing the Letter - A

Practice Writing the Letter - K

Practice Writing the Letter - R

Happy Halloween!

Congratulations, Little Explorer!

You've completed your Halloween adventure with flying colors!

You've sharpened your observation skills, ignited your creativity,

and uncovered hidden treasures on every page. We hope you

had a bewitching time with 'I Spy Halloween.'

Share Your Experience!

Don't forget to share your thoughts with us!

We'd love to hear about your child's adventure. Your feedback

means the world to us and helps other parents discover the magic

of this book.

Share your thoughts and inspire others to embark

on their Halloween journey too!

Thank You for Reading!

I want to personally thank you for choosing this book and supporting my work. Your purchase means the world to me, and I truly hope this book brought joy and creativity to your Halloween season!

Unlock Exclusive Discounts & Special Offers!

As a thank you for being an awesome reader, I'm offering exclusive discounts on my best-selling books! Just sign up for my email list to unlock:

- 20% off your next book purchase
- Early access to new releases
- Special offers just for subscribers

To claim your discount and discover more exciting reads, simply scan the QR code above!

You'll also receive Free Bonus content and be the first to hear about exciting new books for your family to enjoy!

Keep the Magic Alive!

Thank you for being an amazing reader and for your continued support. I look forward to bringing you more fun and engaging books!

With Heartfelt Appreciation,
[Stella Nightwood]

Made in the USA
Columbia, SC
25 October 2024

44993028R00061